DANGER BELOW!

DANGEROUS TEETH!

MORAY EEL ATTACK

BY JAMES BUCKLEY JR.

ILLUSTRATED BY CASSIE ANDERSON

BEARPORT
PUBLISHING

Minneapolis, Minnesota

BEAR CLAW

Credits

20T © Adrian Nunez/Shutterstock; 20BL © Elena Frolova/Shutterstock; 20BR © Ellen Hui/Shutterstock; 21 © Alexandra HB/Shutterstock; 22T © Redmond Durrell/Alamy; 22B © Wildestanimal/Shutterstock

Produced by Shoreline Publishing Group LLC
Santa Barbara, California
Designer: Patty Kelley
Editorial Director: James Buckley Jr.

DISCLAIMER: This graphic story is a dramatization based on true events. It is intended to give the reader a sense of the narrative rather than a presentation of actual details as they occurred.

Library of Congress Cataloging-in-Publication Data

Names: Buckley, James, Jr., 1963– author. | Anderson, Cassie, illustrator.
Title: Dangerous teeth! : moray eel attack / by James Buckley Jr. ;
   illustrated by Cassie Anderson.
Description: Bear claw edition. | Minneapolis, Minnesota : Bearport
   Publishing, [2021] | Series: Danger below! | Includes bibliographical
   references and index.
Identifiers: LCCN 2020008614 (print) | LCCN 2020008615 (ebook) | ISBN
   9781647470517 (library binding) | ISBN 9781647470586 (paperback) | ISBN
   9781647470654 (ebook)
Subjects: LCSH: Morays—Juvenile literature. | Morays—Comic books, strips,
   etc. | Graphic novels.
Classification: LCC QL638.M875 B83 2021 (print) | LCC QL638.M875 (ebook)
   | DDC 597/.43—dc23
LC record available at https://lccn.loc.gov/2020008614
LC ebook record available at https://lccn.loc.gov/2020008615

For more information, write to Bearport Publishing, 5357 Penn Avenue South, Minneapolis, MN 55419. Printed in the United States of America.

CONTENTS

CHAPTER 1

OFF TO FEED AN EEL

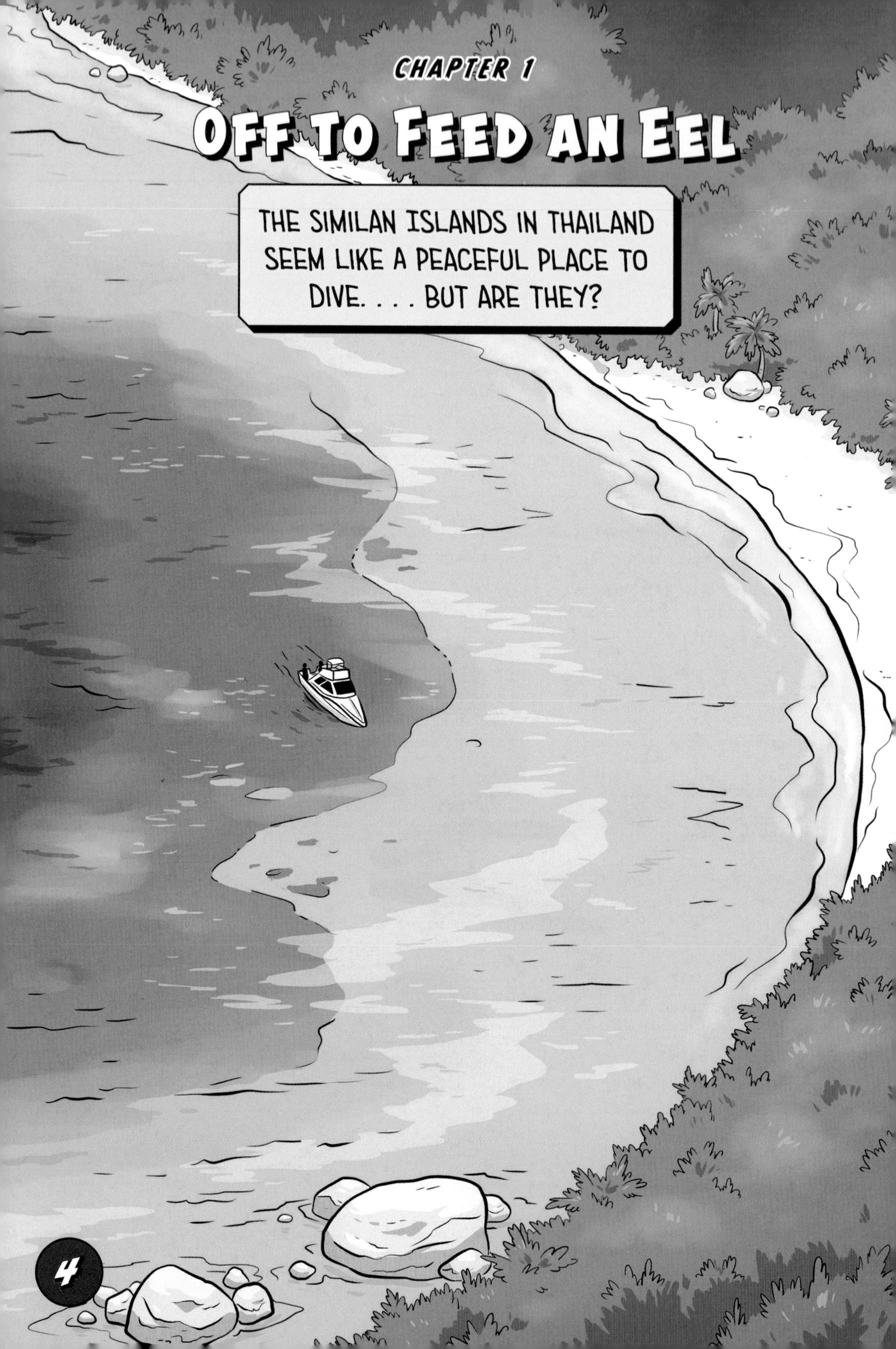
THE SIMILAN ISLANDS IN THAILAND SEEM LIKE A PEACEFUL PLACE TO DIVE. . . . BUT ARE THEY?

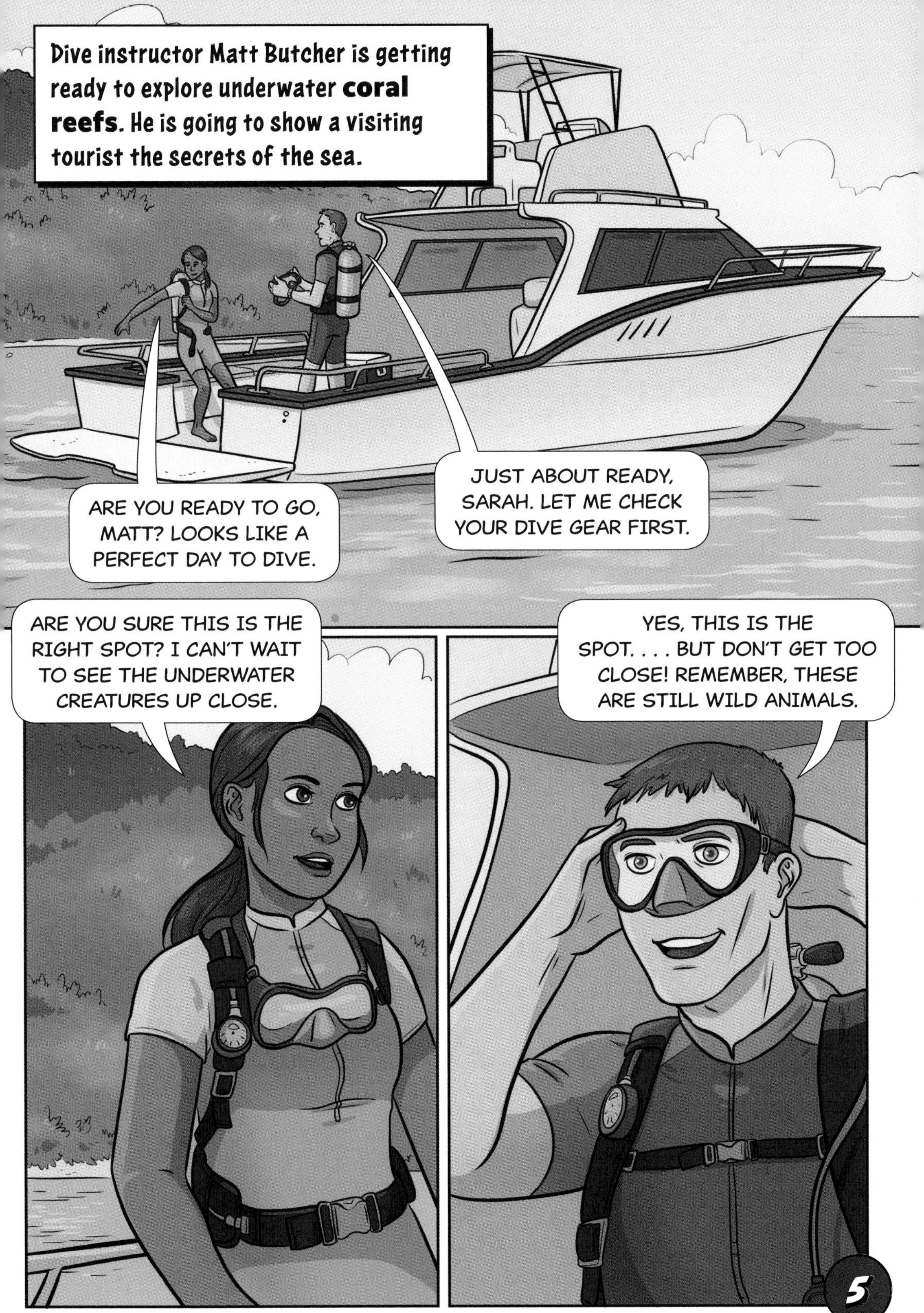
Dive instructor Matt Butcher is getting ready to explore underwater **coral reefs**. He is going to show a visiting tourist the secrets of the sea.
ARE YOU READY TO GO, MATT? LOOKS LIKE A PERFECT DAY TO DIVE.
JUST ABOUT READY, SARAH. LET ME CHECK YOUR DIVE GEAR FIRST.
ARE YOU SURE THIS IS THE RIGHT SPOT? I CAN'T WAIT TO SEE THE UNDERWATER CREATURES UP CLOSE.
YES, THIS IS THE SPOT. . . . BUT DON'T GET TOO CLOSE! REMEMBER, THESE ARE STILL WILD ANIMALS.

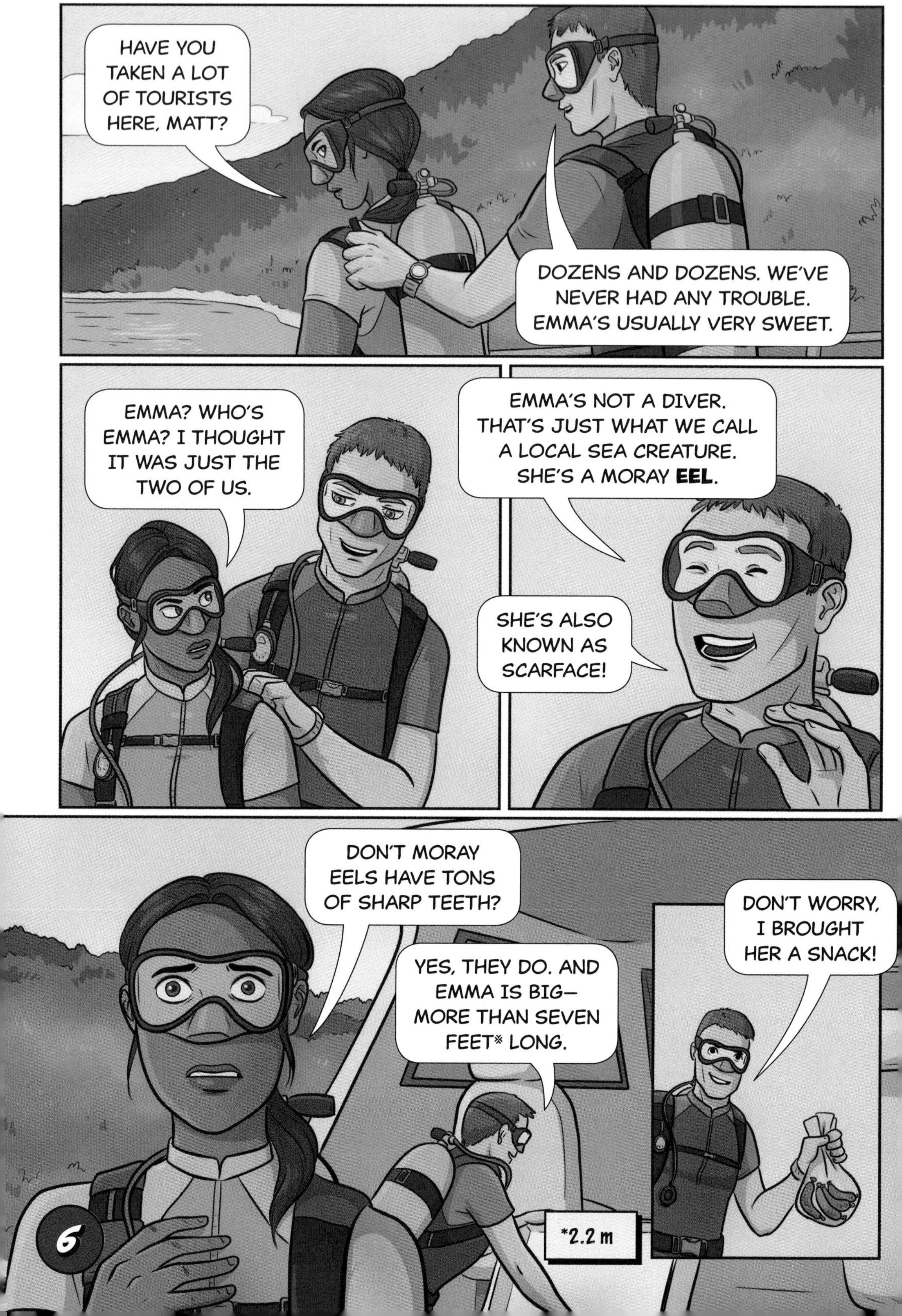
HAVE YOU TAKEN A LOT OF TOURISTS HERE, MATT?
DOZENS AND DOZENS. WE'VE NEVER HAD ANY TROUBLE. EMMA'S USUALLY VERY SWEET.
EMMA? WHO'S EMMA? I THOUGHT IT WAS JUST THE TWO OF US.
EMMA'S NOT A DIVER. THAT'S JUST WHAT WE CALL A LOCAL SEA CREATURE. SHE'S A MORAY **EEL**.
SHE'S ALSO KNOWN AS SCARFACE!
DON'T MORAY EELS HAVE TONS OF SHARP TEETH?
YES, THEY DO. AND EMMA IS BIG— MORE THAN SEVEN FEET* LONG.
DON'T WORRY, I BROUGHT HER A SNACK!
*2.2 m

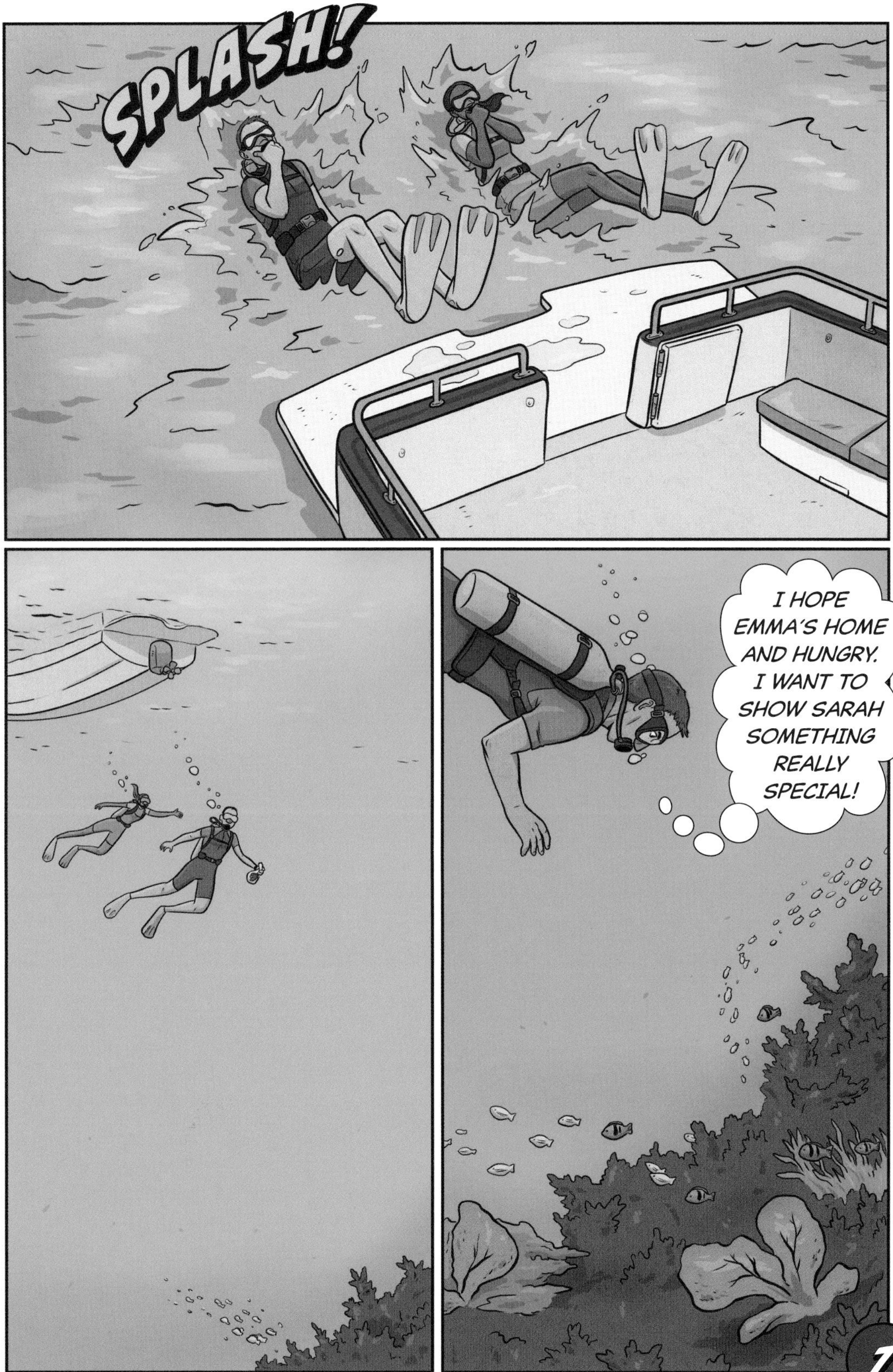
SPLASH!
I HOPE EMMA'S HOME AND HUNGRY. I WANT TO SHOW SARAH SOMETHING REALLY SPECIAL!

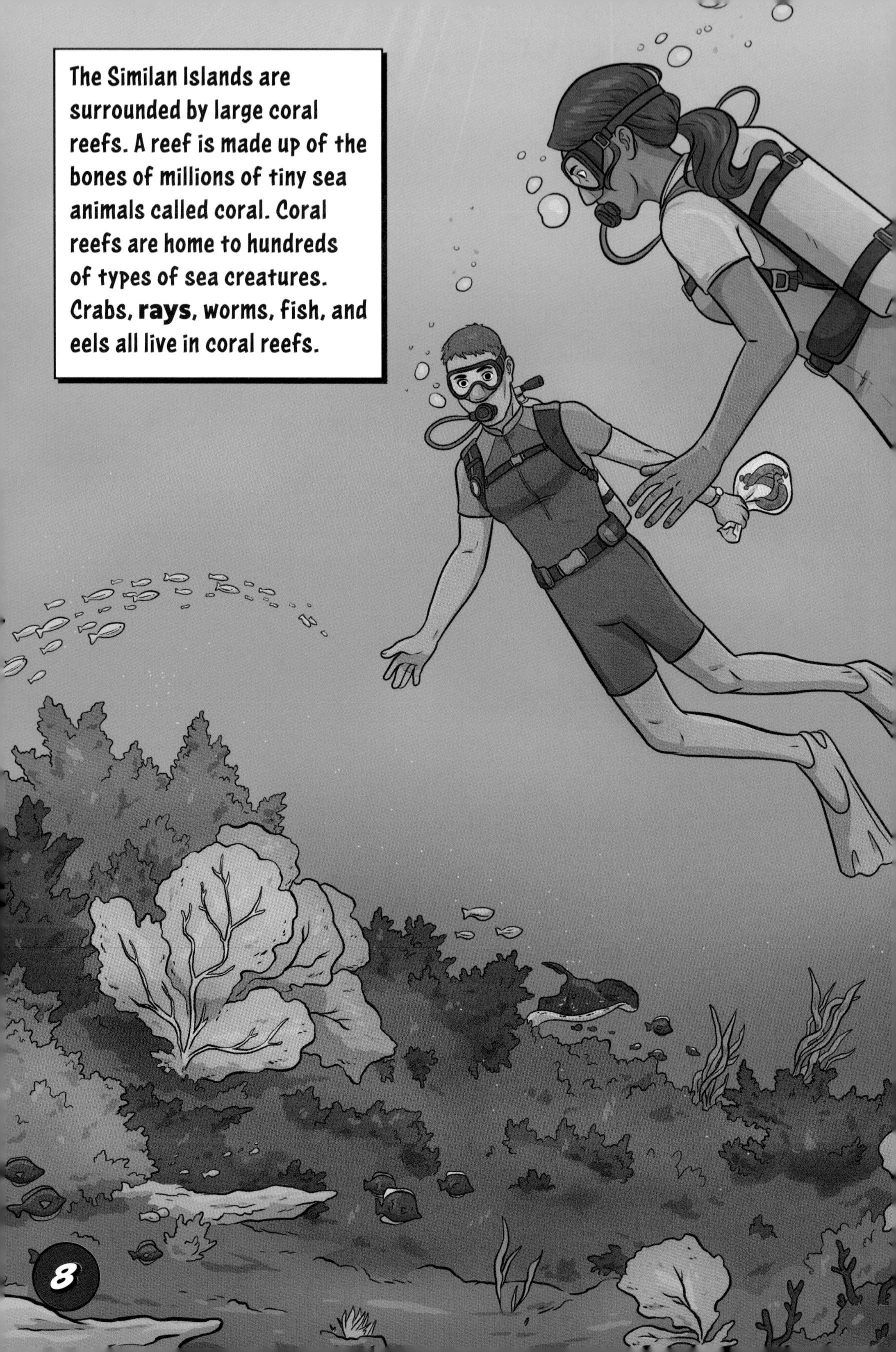
The Similan Islands are surrounded by large coral reefs. A reef is made up of the bones of millions of tiny sea animals called coral. Coral reefs are home to hundreds of types of sea creatures. Crabs, **rays**, worms, fish, and eels all live in coral reefs.

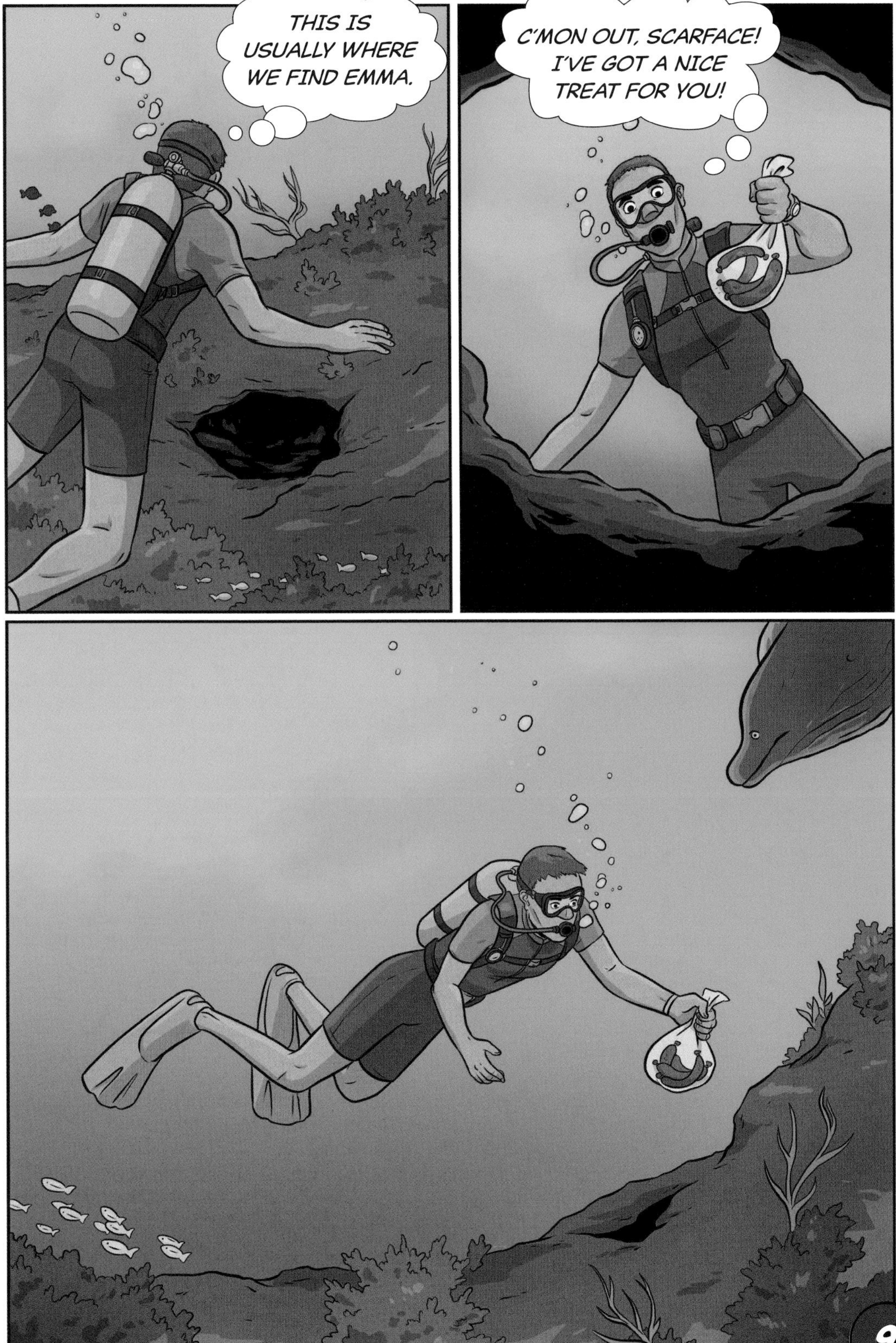
THIS IS USUALLY WHERE WE FIND EMMA.
C'MON OUT, SCARFACE! I'VE GOT A NICE TREAT FOR YOU!

CHAPTER 2

SCARFACE STRIKES!

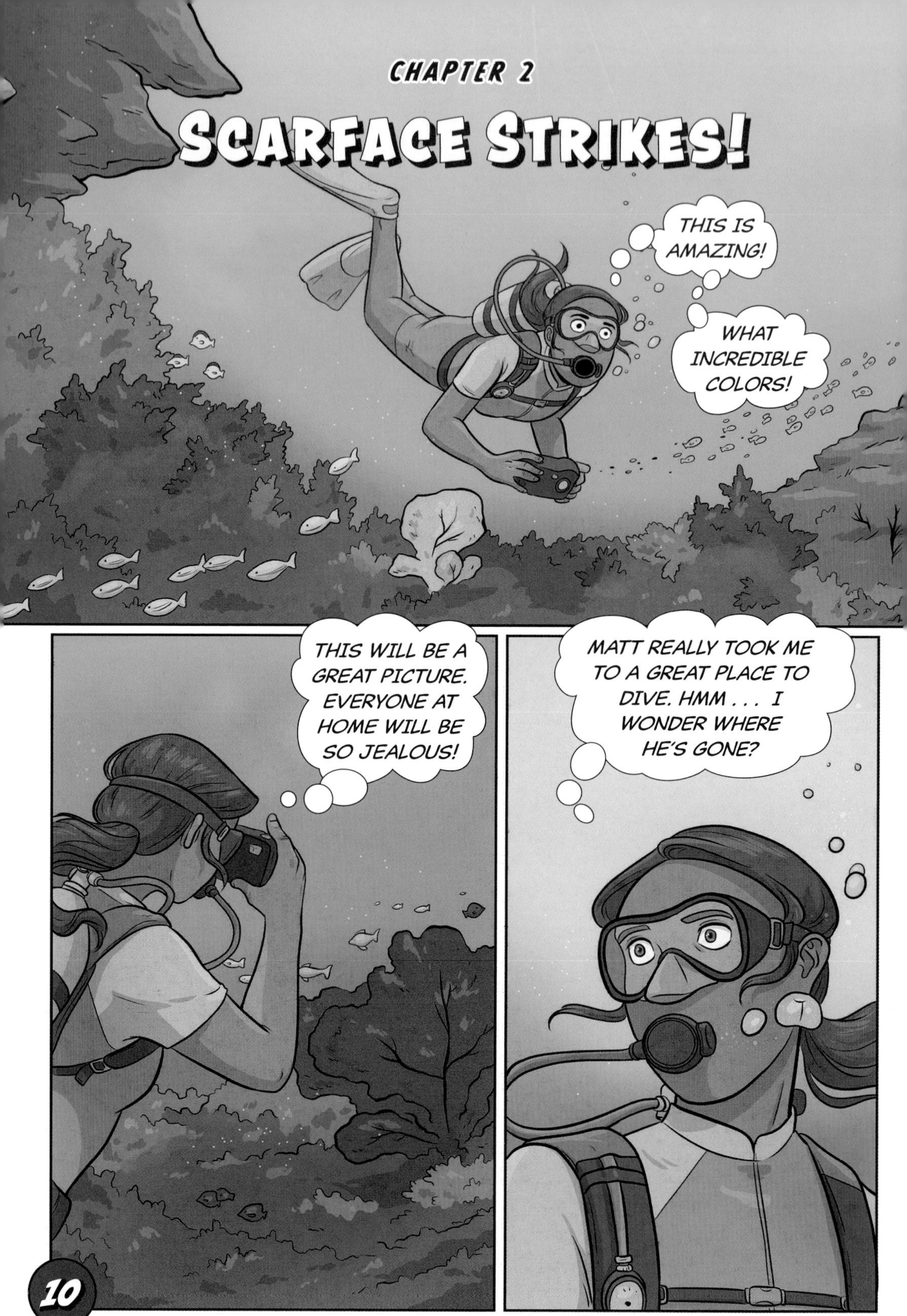
THIS IS AMAZING!
WHAT INCREDIBLE COLORS!
THIS WILL BE A GREAT PICTURE. EVERYONE AT HOME WILL BE SO JEALOUS!
MATT REALLY TOOK ME TO A GREAT PLACE TO DIVE. HMM . . . I WONDER WHERE HE'S GONE?

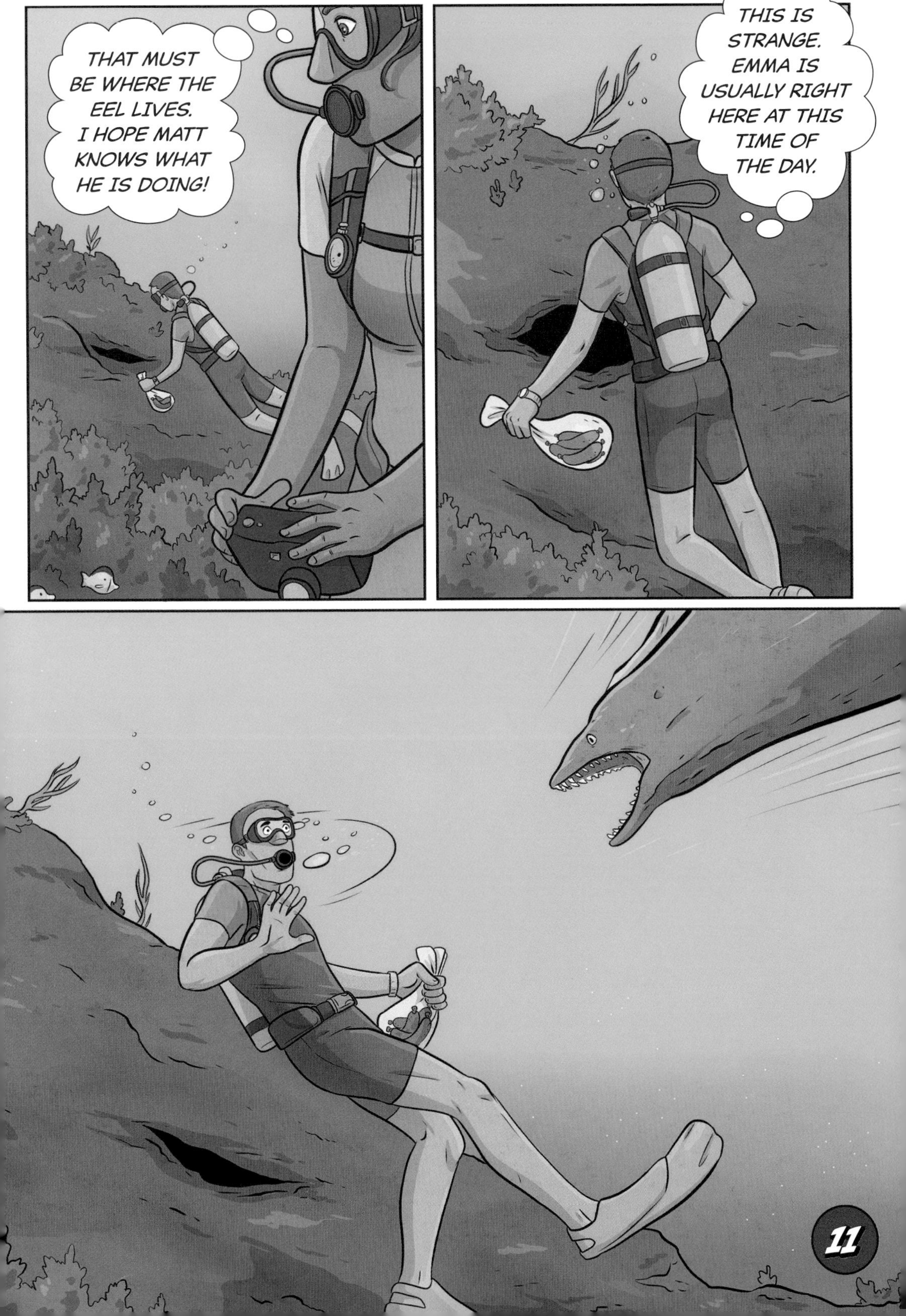
THAT MUST BE WHERE THE EEL LIVES. I HOPE MATT KNOWS WHAT HE IS DOING!
THIS IS STRANGE. EMMA IS USUALLY RIGHT HERE AT THIS TIME OF THE DAY.

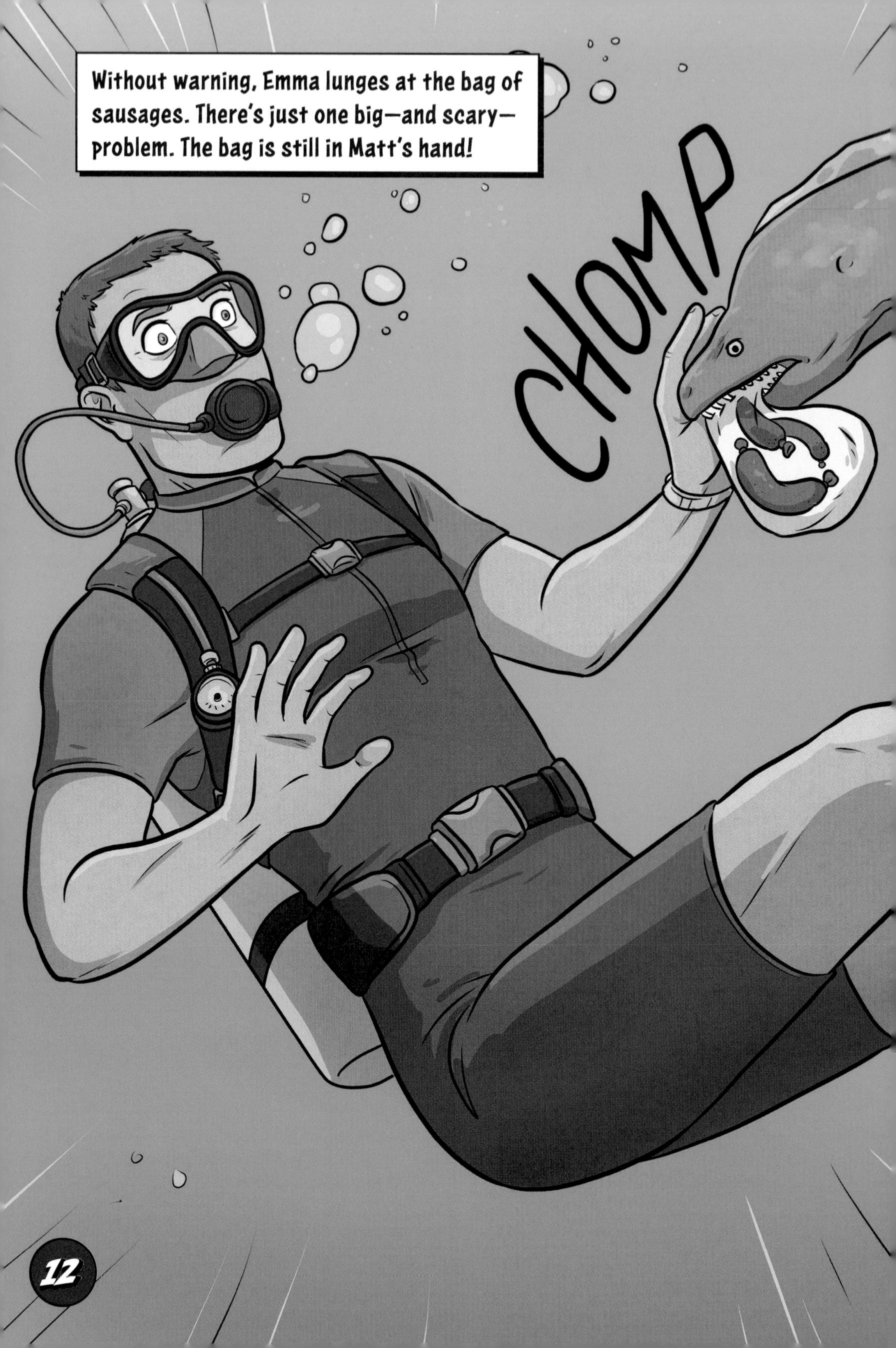
Without warning, Emma lunges at the bag of sausages. There's just one big—and scary—problem. The bag is still in Matt's hand!
CHOMP

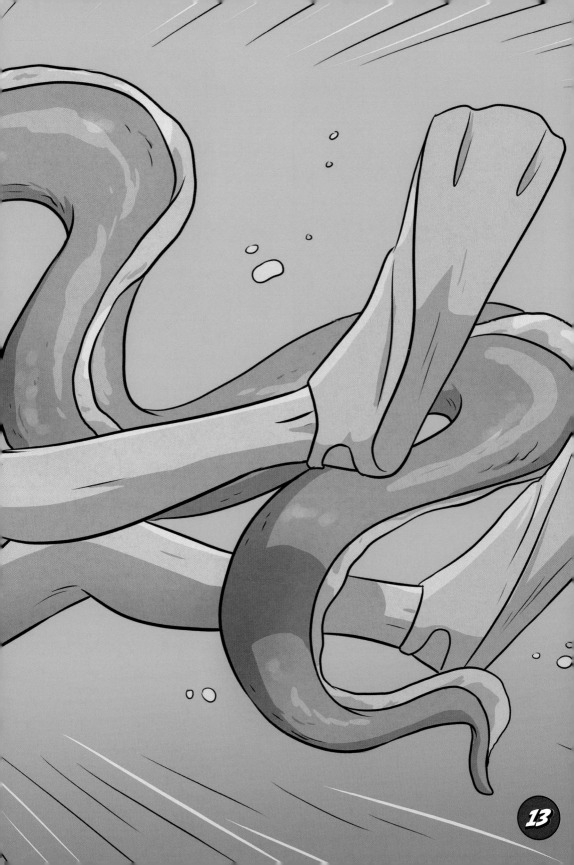

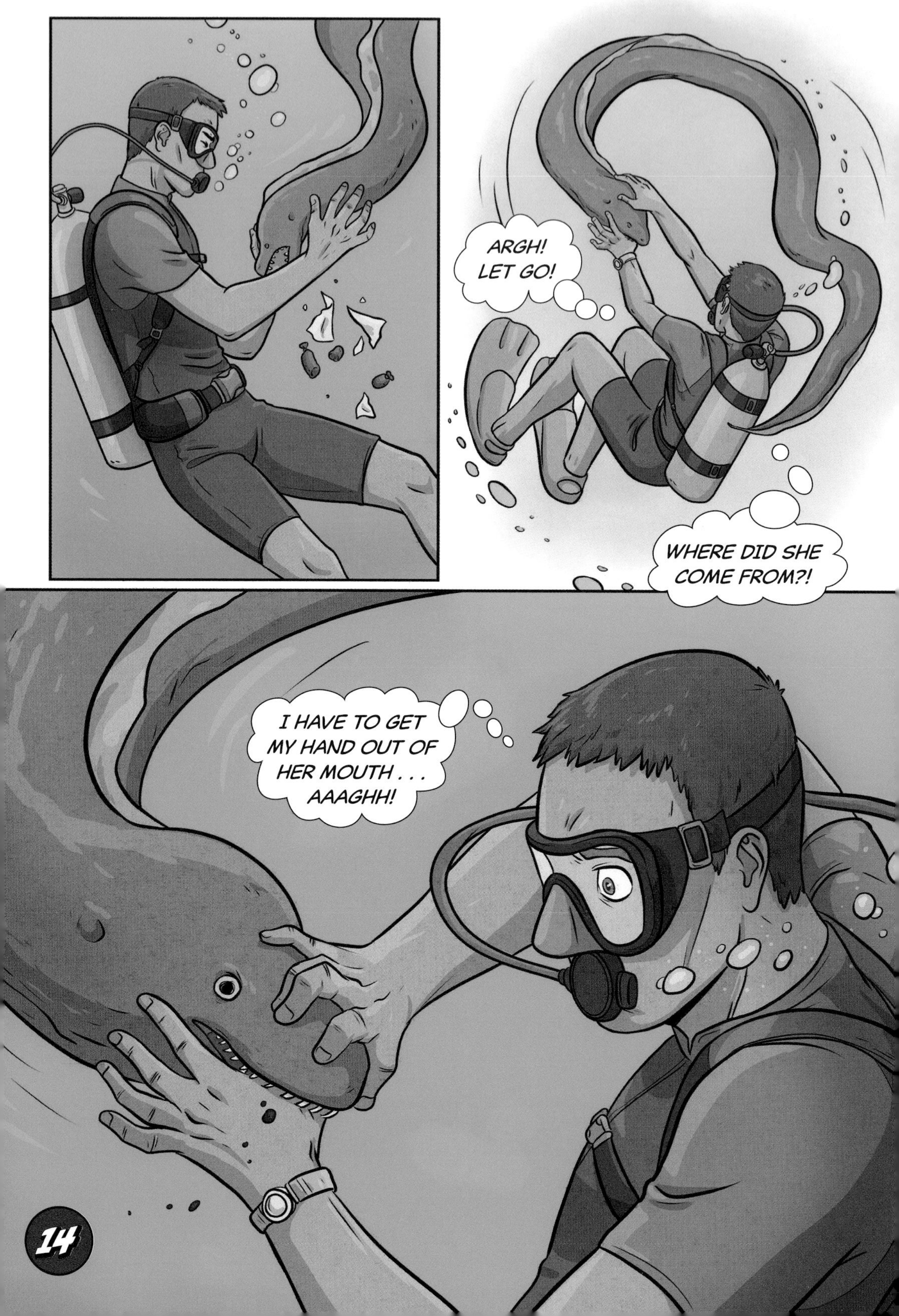
ARGH! LET GO!
WHERE DID SHE COME FROM?!
I HAVE TO GET MY HAND OUT OF HER MOUTH . . . AAAGHH!

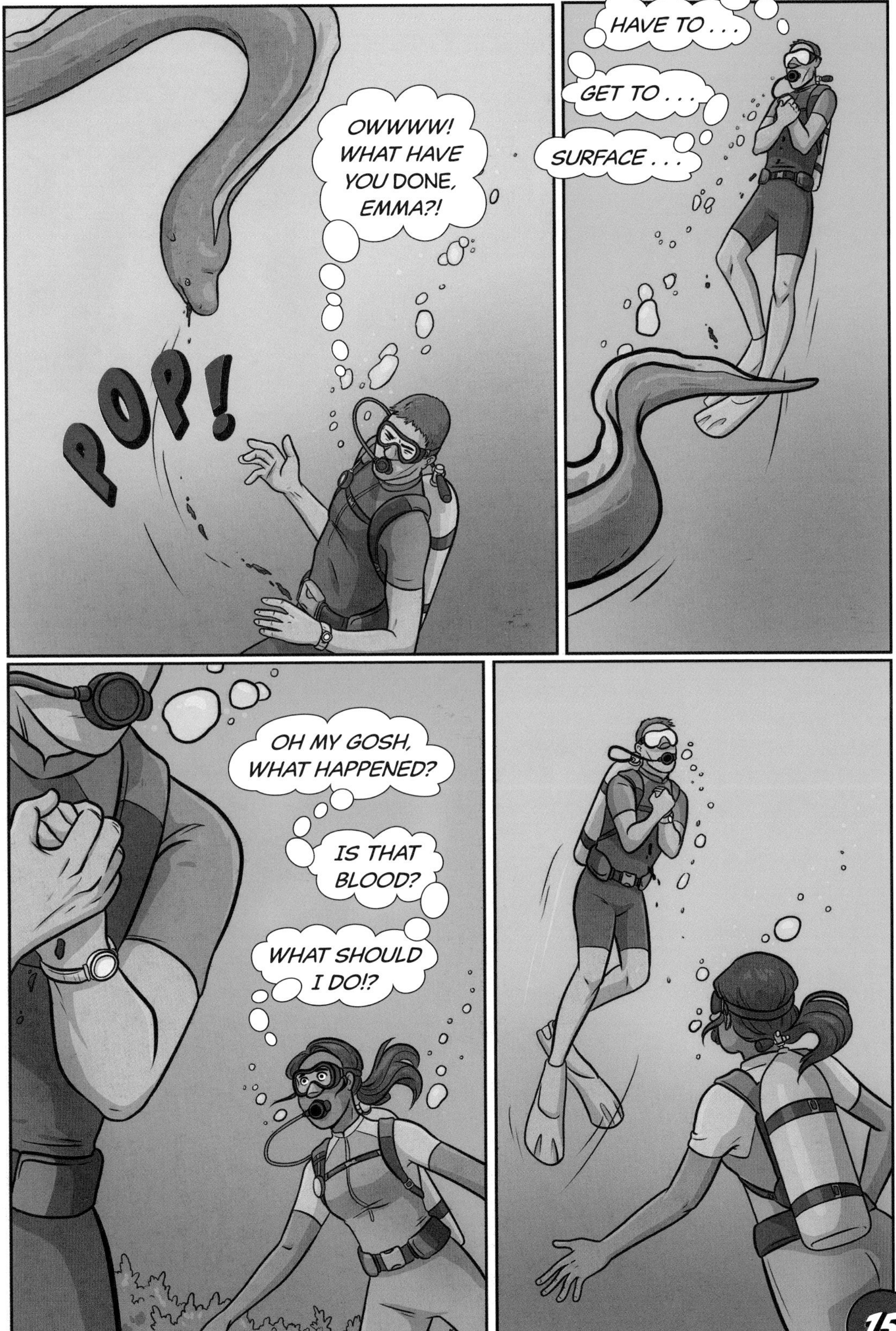
OWWWW! WHAT HAVE YOU DONE, EMMA?!
POP!
HAVE TO . . .
GET TO . . .
SURFACE . . .
OH MY GOSH, WHAT HAPPENED?
IS THAT BLOOD?
WHAT SHOULD I DO!?

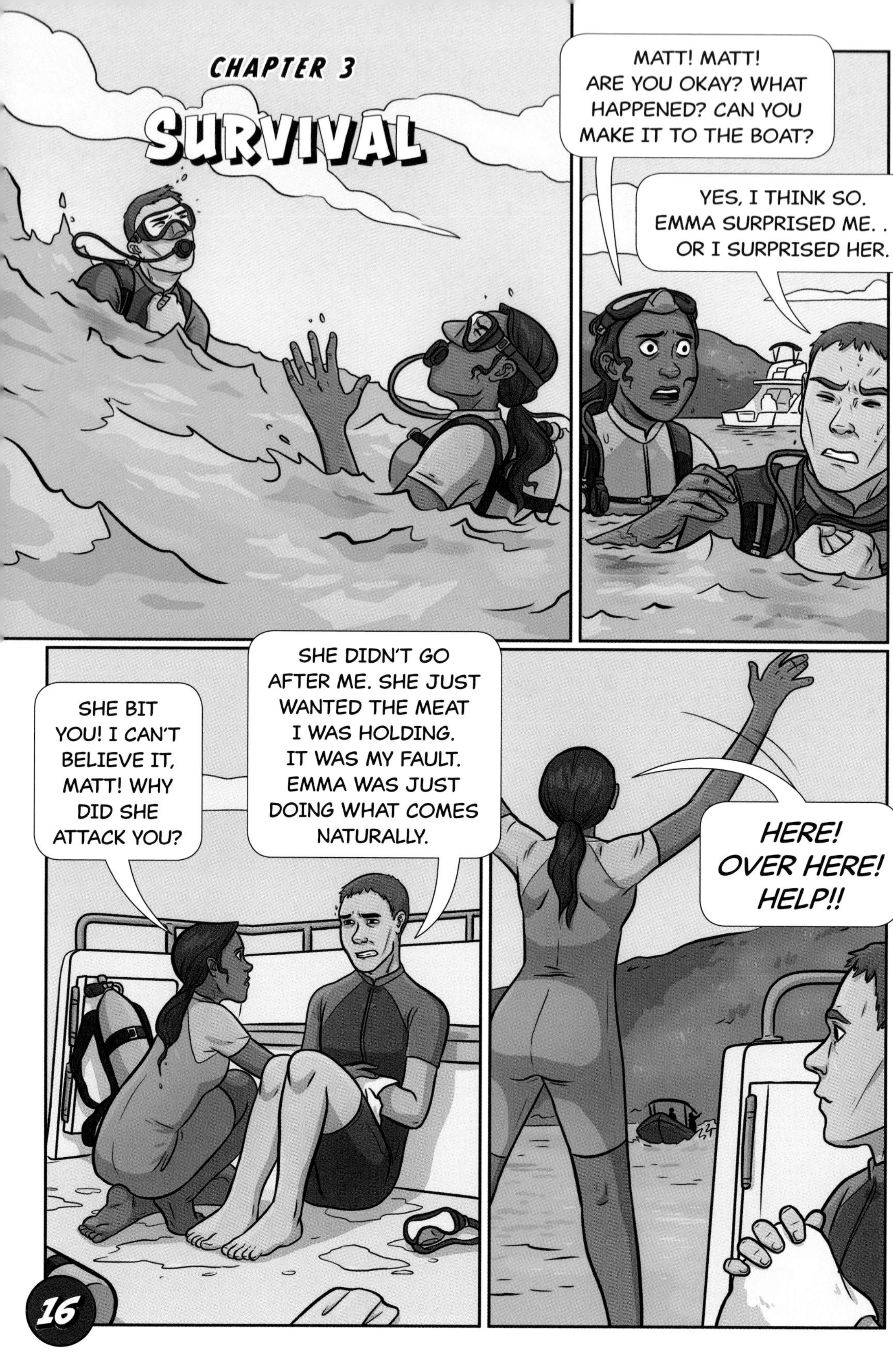
CHAPTER 3
SURVIVAL
MATT! MATT! ARE YOU OKAY? WHAT HAPPENED? CAN YOU MAKE IT TO THE BOAT?
YES, I THINK SO. EMMA SURPRISED ME. . . . OR I SURPRISED HER.
SHE BIT YOU! I CAN'T BELIEVE IT, MATT! WHY DID SHE ATTACK YOU?
SHE DIDN'T GO AFTER ME. SHE JUST WANTED THE MEAT I WAS HOLDING. IT WAS MY FAULT. EMMA WAS JUST DOING WHAT COMES NATURALLY.
HERE! OVER HERE! HELP!!

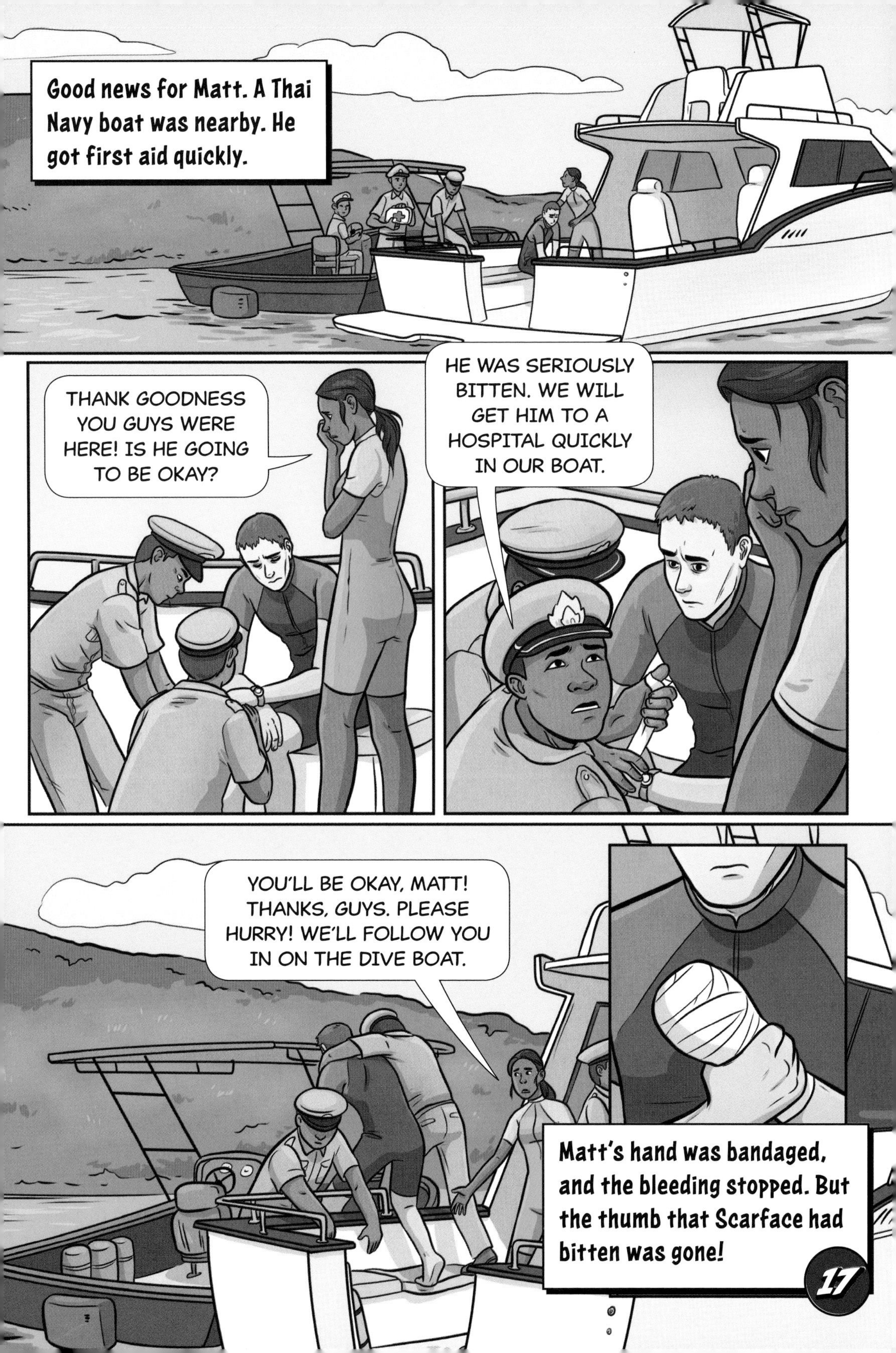
Good news for Matt. A Thai Navy boat was nearby. He got first aid quickly.
THANK GOODNESS YOU GUYS WERE HERE! IS HE GOING TO BE OKAY?
HE WAS SERIOUSLY BITTEN. WE WILL GET HIM TO A HOSPITAL QUICKLY IN OUR BOAT.
YOU'LL BE OKAY, MATT! THANKS, GUYS. PLEASE HURRY! WE'LL FOLLOW YOU IN ON THE DIVE BOAT.
Matt's hand was bandaged, and the bleeding stopped. But the thumb that Scarface had bitten was gone!

News of the accident spread throughout the local dive community.

AND THEN WHAT HAPPENED, MR. BUTCHER?

I COULDN'T GET MY THUMB OUT OF HER MOUTH ONCE SHE STARTED BITING. THE TEETH OF A MORAY ARE ANGLED BACKWARD, SO SHE GOT A BETTER GRIP ON MY THUMB WITH EVERY BITE.

I TRIED PUSHING THE FINGERS OF MY RIGHT HAND INTO HER MOUTH TO FORCE HER TO OPEN IT, BUT SHE WOULDN'T LET GO. SHE COULD TASTE BLOOD BY THEN.

SHE WAS SHAKING HER HEAD FROM SIDE TO SIDE, BITING HARDER ALL THE TIME. FIVE SECONDS LATER— *POP!* MY THUMB JUST CAME OFF.

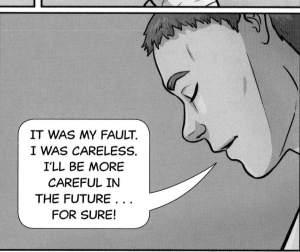

IT WAS MY FAULT. I WAS CARELESS. I'LL BE MORE CAREFUL IN THE FUTURE . . . FOR SURE!

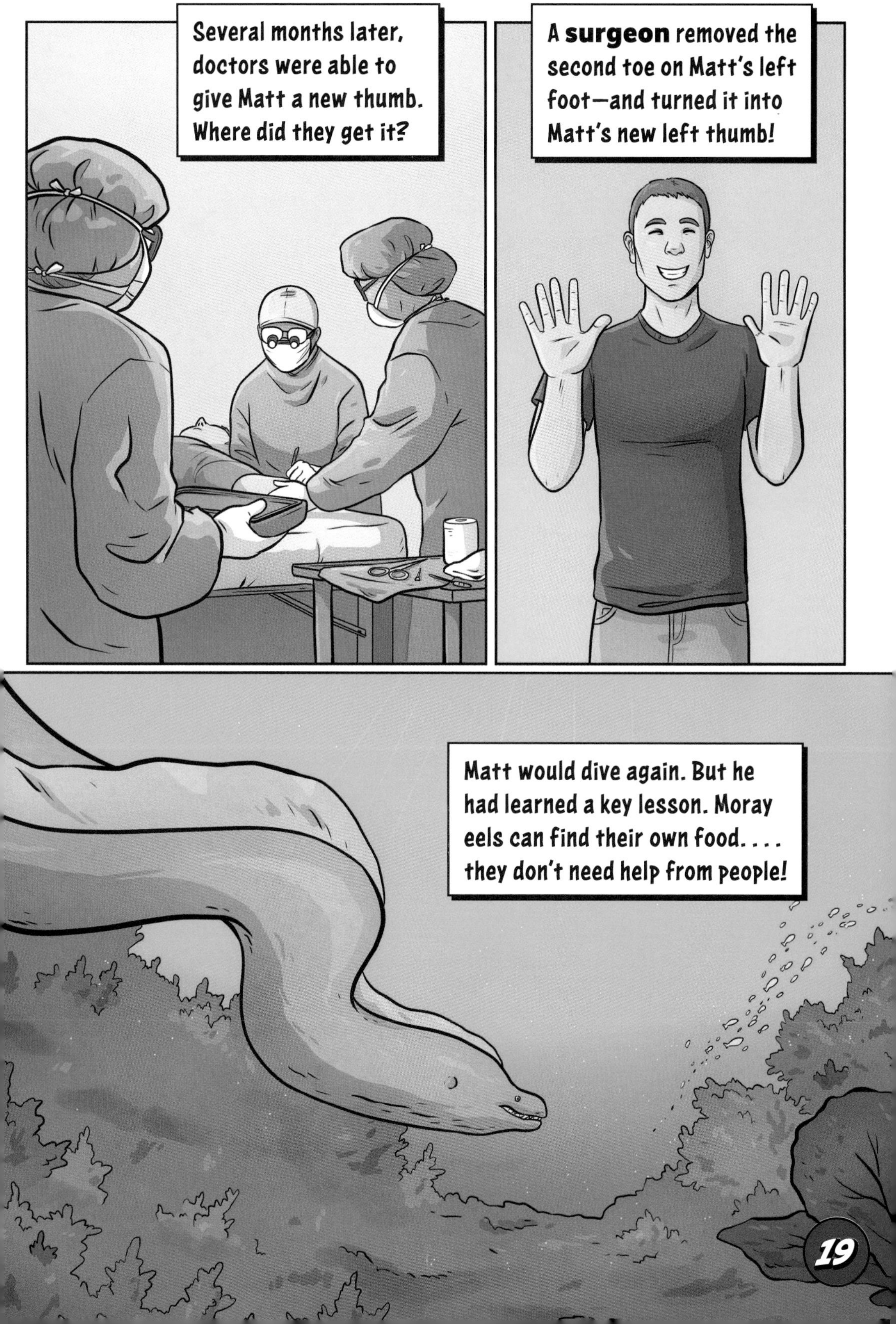
Several months later, doctors were able to give Matt a new thumb. Where did they get it?
A surgeon removed the second toe on Matt's left foot—and turned it into Matt's new left thumb!
Matt would dive again. But he had learned a key lesson. Moray eels can find their own food. . . . they don't need help from people!

ABOUT MORAY EELS

Moray eels are a type of fish that live in warm oceans around the world. There are more than 200 **species** of moray eels. Almost all of them have large mouths with very sharp teeth. Moray eels usually don't chase after their **prey**. Instead, they wait and lunge out when prey swims past. Though the diver in this story was attacked, moray eels generally don't attack people.

MORAY EELS

- Moray eels range in size from 8 inches (20 cm) to more than 13 feet (4 m) long.

- Some moray eels can weigh more than 80 pounds (36 kg).

- These eels eat fish, squid, octopuses, crabs, and shrimp.

- A moray eel has one main fin that stretches the length of its body.

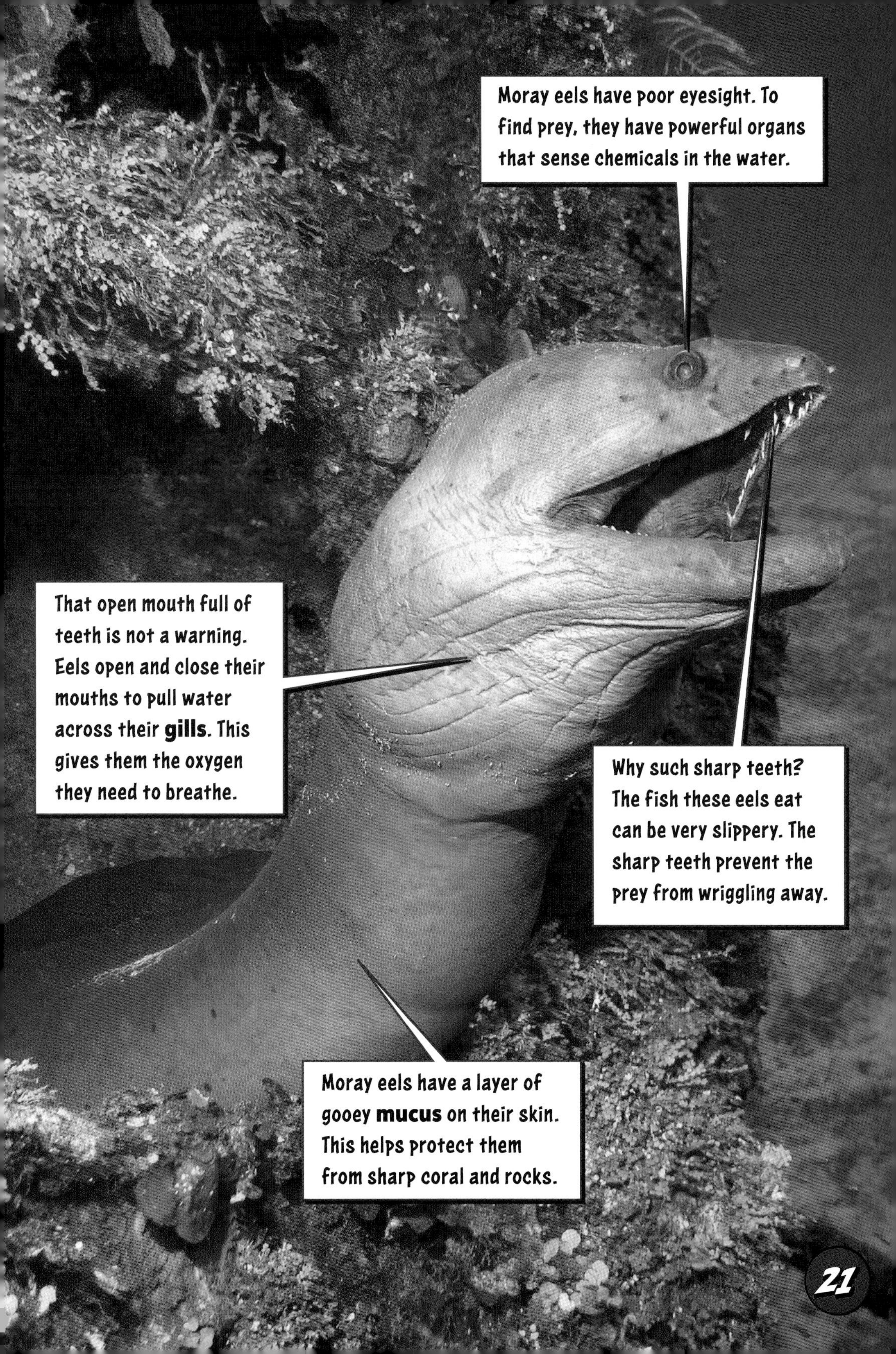
Moray eels have poor eyesight. To find prey, they have powerful organs that sense chemicals in the water.
That open mouth full of teeth is not a warning. Eels open and close their mouths to pull water across their **gills**. This gives them the oxygen they need to breathe.
Why such sharp teeth? The fish these eels eat can be very slippery. The sharp teeth prevent the prey from wriggling away.
Moray eels have a layer of gooey **mucus** on their skin. This helps protect them from sharp coral and rocks.

OTHER WATER CREATURES THAT BITE!

The moray eel is one swimmer with a powerful bite.
These fish also have painful and dangerous bites.

PIRANHAS

- These small freshwater fish live in South American rivers. They're known for their razor-sharp teeth and strong bite.
- Piranhas often travel in groups and are known to attack much larger animals.
- Piranhas rarely bite people. They usually feed on other fish, insects, snakes, and even some small mammals.

SHARKS

- More people are bitten by sharks than any other type of fish. However, deaths from shark attacks are still very rare. A person is more likely to be attacked and killed by a dog than by a shark.

- Great white, bull, and tiger sharks are most often involved in attacks on humans.
- Humans hunt and kill sharks, which is the greatest threat to these fish.

GLOSSARY

coral reefs underwater structures made of living and dead animals called polyps

eel a slender snakelike fish

gills body parts used by fish and other undersea animals to breathe

mucus a slippery coating found on many types of fish

prey animals that are hunted by other animals for food

rays sea creatures with wide, triangular wings and long, thin tails

species closely related groups of animals

surgeon a doctor who performs operations

INDEX

READ MORE

Green, Jen. *Moray Eel (The Deep End, Animal Life Underwater).* New York: Bearport Publishing (2010).

Niver, Heather Moore. *20 Fun Facts About Moray Eels (Fun Fact File: Fierce Fish).* New York: Gareth Stevens (2013).

Shaffer, Lindsay. *Moray Eels (Animals of the Coral Reef).* Minneapolis: Bellwether Media (2020).

LEARN MORE ONLINE

1. Go to **www.factsurfer.com**

2. Enter "**Dangerous Teeth**" into the search box.

3. Click on the cover of this book to see a list of websites.